Olympic Champions

By Lynne Blanche and Claire Daniel

Series Literacy Consultant
Dr Ros Fisher

Pearson Education Limited
Edinburgh Gate
Harlow
Essex CM20 2JE
England

www.longman.co.uk

ISBN 0 582 84552 1

Colour reproduction by Colourscan, Singapore
Printed and bound in China by Leo Paper Products Ltd.

The Publisher's policy is to use paper manufactured from sustainable forests.

The following people from **DK** have
contributed to the development of this product:
Art Director Rachael Foster

Carole Oliver, Nick Avery **Design**	**Managing Editor** Scarlett O'Hara
Helen McFarland **Picture Research**	**Editorial** Kate Pearce, Amanda Rayner
Ed Merritt **Cartography**	**Production** Rosalind Holmes
Richard Czapnik, Andy Smith **Cover Design**	**DTP** David McDonald
Consultant Norman Barrett	

Dorling Kindersley would like to thank: Tanni Grey-Thompson for the image on page 15, Marc Gagnon for the images on pages 10, 11 and 12, Johnny Pau for additional cover design work.

Picture Credits: Action Plus: Robb Coxx/STL/Icon 4cl; Glyn Kirk 1; Philippe Millereau/DPPI 12cl. AKG London: Erich Lessing 4tl. Associated Press AP: 27tr; Denis Paquin 25b. Camera Press: David Dyson 17t. Corbis: Bettmann 7cr; Duomo 9cr; Jon Hicks 18b; Kit Houghton 3; Rick Maiman 28tl; Neal Preston 26tl, 27br, 27l, 28bl, 29br; Jean-Yves Rusniewski/TempSport 22tl, 25tr; Orban Thierry/Sygma 21b; Karl Weatherly 5tr. Empics Ltd: DPA/DPA 23t; Tony Marshall 14bc; Steve Mitchell 23cr; 30b; Neal Simpson 8–9, 19r; Valeria Witters/WITTERS 4b, 5b. Getty Images: 16; Adam Pretty 30tl; 31br; Simon Bruty 24–25; Robert Cianflone 6tl; Tony Feder 9tl; 31br; Mike Hewitt 20t; Christopher Lee 17br; Bob Martin 22tl, 29t; Donald Miralle 10tl, 13br; Mike Powell 11b; Craig Prentis/Stringer 16br; 13br; Jamie Squire 14–15, 15tr; Michael Steele 18tl; Michale Steele 19tl. Newspix Archive/Nationwide News: 7tl; Brett Faulkner 6-7. Pa Photos: Ian West 14tl. Jacket: Action Plus: Glyn Kirk front t; Empics Ltd: Matthew Ashton front bl. Getty Images: Mike Powell back.

All other images: DK Dorling Kindersley © 2004. For further information see www.dkimages.com
Dorling Kindersley Ltd., 80 Strand, London WC2R ORL

Contents

Olympic Dreams

an athlete throwing a javelin

Olympic medals

In 776 BC the first Olympic Games was held in Greece. It started with only one running race. However, over the years new events were added. These events included chariot races, more running races, wrestling and discus throwing. Then in AD 394 the Emperor banned the Olympic Games.

In 1896 the Olympic Games was restarted. It was held in Greece. More than 300 men competed in over forty events.

Today the Olympic Games is still very popular. It is a great honour to take part in the event. Thousand of athletes come from all over the world to compete. There are hundreds of events now. These include running races, swimming, discus throwing and gymnastics.

Athletes train for many years before taking part in the Olympic Games. Often they start training as young children. This book looks at the lives and achievements of six Olympic champions.

The Olympic flag

In 1996, athletes from all over the world competed at the Olympics in Atlanta, Georgia.

Name:
Catherine Freeman

Birthdate:
16th February 1973

Birthplace: Mackay,
Queensland, Australia

Sport: Athletics

Olympic Medals:
1 silver in 1996;
1 gold in 2000

AUSTRALIA

Mackay
Queensland

Map Key
◉ Town

N
W — E
S

Cathy Freeman was born in 1973 in Australia. She was one of five children. Her father was a talented rugby player called Norman Freeman.

Cathy started running when she was very young. By the time she was eight years old she had won many races. Cathy's family were very proud of her. She had a sign on her door that said, "I am the world's greatest athlete".

Cathy Freeman lights the Olympic flame for the 2000 Olympics.

Cathy aged eleven years old

Cathy continued to win lots of races. When she was fifteen years old she proved she was one of the best runners in the country. People were impressed with her running at the Australian schools championships. Then in 1990 Cathy showed she was one of the best runners in the world. She represented Australia in the World Junior Games in Bulgaria.

The Olympic Flame

The Olympic flame is lit by a torch at the opening of the Games. Carrying the torch is a great honour. People take turns carrying the torch from Olympia, Greece, to the city where the Olympics is being held.

That same year Cathy went to the 1990 Commonwealth Games. There she ran as part of the 100-metre relay team. She and her team won the gold medal. Cathy was named Young Australian of the Year for this achievement.

Two years later Cathy went to the 1992 Olympics in Barcelona, Spain. However, this time she didn't win a medal.

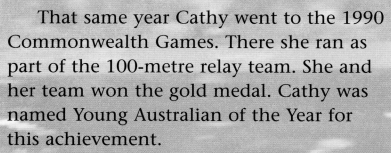

Cathy in the women's 400-metre final at the 2000 Olympics in Sydney

Cathy Freeman is a role model for young athletes all over the world.

In 1996 Cathy returned to the Olympic Games in Atlanta in the United States. This time she won a silver medal.

Four years later Cathy lit the Olympic flame. This marked the start of the 2000 Olympics in Sydney, Australia. Cathy won the 400-metre race in her own country. She was delighted when she was awarded the gold medal. She had finally achieved her goal.

Cathy won a gold medal at the 2000 Olympics.

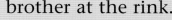
Marc Gagnon leads in a speed skating race at the 2002 Winter Olympics.

Marc Gagnon

Marc Gagnon was born in 1975 in Canada. He had an older brother called Sylvain who was a talented skater. Marc often went to the skating rink with his family. His parents coached Sylvain while Marc watched from the side. Marc wanted to try skating, too, so when he was only three years old he joined his brother at the rink.

Marc at four years old

A year later Marc entered his first big race. He was just four years old. Marc showed that he was as talented as his older brother. Over the years the brothers continued skating.

In 1990 Marc was selected for the Canadian national team. Then in 1992 he showed he was the best skater in the world when he won his first World Championship. He was just seventeen years old.

Marc celebrates with his family.

Marc leading in a speed-skating race

Marc at the skating rink

Olympic Training

Athletes train for many years before taking part in the Olympics. Many training centres have been built around the world to help athletes of all levels, including Olympians. Athletes visit these centres to receive expert training and coaching.

Two years later Marc skated at the 1994 Winter Olympics in Lillehammer, Norway. There he won the bronze medal in the 1,000-metre short-track race.

Marc returned to the 1998 Winter Olympics in Nagano, Japan. There he won a gold medal with the short-track relay team.

After the Olympics, Marc was tired and fed up. He decided to stop skating. However, he found it impossible to stay away from the ice. A year later he went back into training for the next Olympics.

After three years of hard work, Marc was ready. He arrived full of excitement at the 2002 Winter Olympics in Salt Lake City in the United States.

All Marc's hard work paid off. First he won the bronze medal in the 1,500-metre race. Then he went on to win the gold medal for the 500-metre race. Finally he won the gold medal for the 5,000-metre relay race. His Olympic dream had come true. Marc was a winner.

Marc (middle) at the 2002 Olympics

Name:
Tanni Grey-Thompson

Birthdate:
26th July 1969

Birthplace: Cardiff, Wales

Sport:
Wheelchair track

Olympic Medals:
4 gold in 1992;
1 gold in 1996;
4 gold in 2000

Tanni Grey-Thompson

Tanni Grey-Thompson was born in 1969 in Cardiff. She was born with spina bifida which is a disease of the spine. This stopped her from walking, but not from trying new things.

When Tanni was young, she loved watching the London Marathon on television. She told her mother that she would race in the marathon one day.

Tanni loved sports. She played wheelchair basketball and tennis. She swam and did archery, too.

As a girl, Tanni made lots of friends at Brownies.

The Paralympic Games

The Paralympic Games are for athletes who have physical challenges. The Games are held in the same years as the Olympics and in the same cities.

Tanni's favourite sport was wheelchair racing. She raced for the first time when she was thirteen years old. She did so well that she decided she wanted to race in the Paralympics.

Tanni trained very hard to be fit enough for the Paralympics. She also kept playing tennis and basketball. Tanni was determined to reach her goal no matter how long it took.

Tanni trains in a custom-built wheelchair.

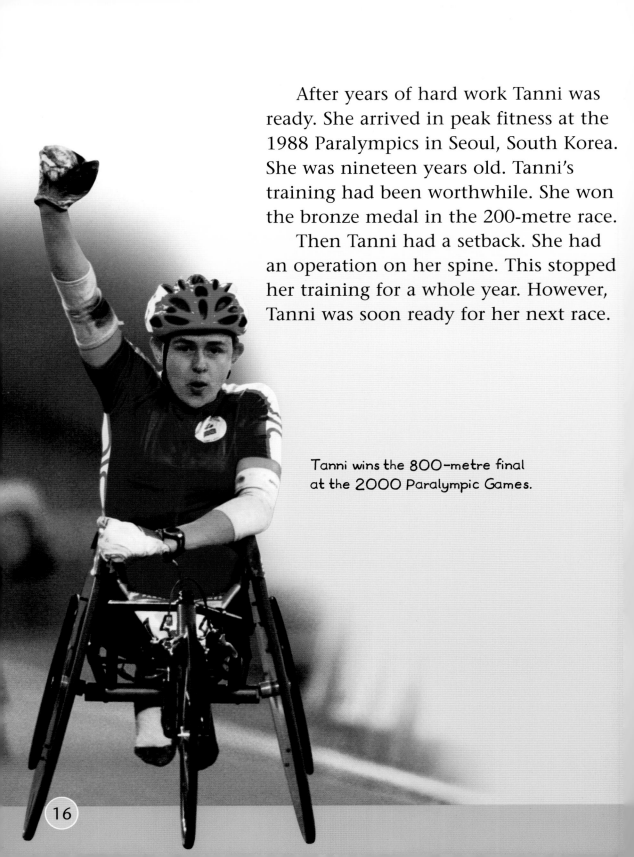

After years of hard work Tanni was ready. She arrived in peak fitness at the 1988 Paralympics in Seoul, South Korea. She was nineteen years old. Tanni's training had been worthwhile. She won the bronze medal in the 200-metre race.

Then Tanni had a setback. She had an operation on her spine. This stopped her training for a whole year. However, Tanni was soon ready for her next race.

Tanni wins the 800-metre final at the 2000 Paralympic Games.

Tanni with some of her medals from the Paralympics

Tanni raced in the 1992 Paralympics in Barcelona, Spain. There she won four gold medals. That same year she raced in the London Marathon and came first. There was no stopping her. Tanni went on to win the London Marathon six more times.

Next Tanni raced at the 1996 Paralympics in Atlanta in the United States and the 2000 Paralympics in Sydney, Australia. She won even more gold medals. Tanni's determination had been rewarded.

Tanni speaks at a conference in Monaco, 2003.

Name:
Haile Gebreselassie

Birthdate:
18th April 1973

Birthplace:
Arssi, Ethiopia

Sport: Track

Olympic Medals:
1 gold in 1996;
1 gold in 2000

AFRICA

Arssi
Ethiopia

N
W   E
S

Map Key
⊙ Region

Haile Gebreselassie

Haile Gebreselassie was born in 1973 in Ethiopia. He grew up on a farm. Haile loved running. Every day he ran 10 kilometres to school and 10 kilometres home again. He ran around the farm and across the fields, too.

When Haile was seven years old Miruts Yifter won two gold medals at the 1980 Olympics in Moscow, Russia. He was an Ethiopian like Haile. This inspired Haile to race in the Olympics, too.

Haile used to run on hilly, country roads as a child.

Haile's training includes running 29 kilometres a day.

For many years Haile trained hard at running long distances. Then in 1998 he ran in a marathon in Addis Ababa (the capital of Ethiopia). He was fifteen years old. Haile did very well in the race. However, he knew he could run much faster.

Haile continued to train hard. In 1992 he ran in the World Junior Athletics Championships in South Korea. There he won the 5,000-metre race and the 10,000-metre race.

Haile competes in the 3,000-metre race at the World Indoor Championships in France.

Haile (middle) runs in the 10,000-metre final during the 1996 Olympics.

Timing It

Sometimes just a fraction of a second separates runners in track events. Stopwatches, multi-lane timers and automatic timers are used to time the runners. Some electronic starting pistols produce digital photos of the finish.

In 1996 Haile went to the Olympics in Atlanta in the United States. There he ran in the 10,000-metre race with his friend, Paul Tergat. Haile ran behind Paul for most of the race. Then in the last lap he raced ahead and won the gold medal.

Over the next four years Haile set many world records at several distances. He became a popular runner. He was known for his powerful sprint finish and his wide grin.

In 2000 Haile had an ankle injury. This nearly stopped him running in the Olympics in Sydney, Australia. However, he decided to run and raced with his friend Paul Tergat. By the last lap of the 10,000-metre final, he found himself behind Paul again. Haile got a final burst of energy and just beat Paul. It was the closest 10,000-metre win in Olympic history.

Haile (left) winning the 10,000-metre race at the 2000 Olympics.

Pablo Morales

Pablo Morales was born in 1964 in the United States. Pablo's mother had nearly drowned when she was younger. She wanted her children to be safe so they learned to swim when they were very young.

During his swimming lessons Pablo didn't really listen to his teacher because he just wanted to have fun in the water.

Pablo was inspired by Olympic swimmer Mark Spitz (left).

Then in 1972 Pablo joined a swimming team as a beginner. He discovered that his favourite swimming stoke was the butterfly. Soon he showed his talent. At ten years old Pablo was the fastest swimmer at the 100-metre butterfly for his age.

When Pablo was thirteen years old he started training twice a day. Soon he held the record for the fastest swimmer at the 100-metre butterfly in his school.

Pablo's Swim Stroke

The butterfly stroke takes strong arms. The swimmer's arms and shoulders move up over the water as the legs push the body forward.

In 1983 Pablo went to Stanford University. There he won more swimming events than anyone else in the country.

By the next year Pablo was swimming in the 1984 Olympics in Los Angeles in the United States. There he won two silver medals for butterfly races and one gold medal for the 400-metre relay race.

Pablo was very happy with his medals, but he wanted to win the gold medal for the 100-metre race.

Pablo won the gold medal at the 1992 Olympic Games.

In 1987 Pablo went to law school. He took time off in the next year to train for the 1988 Olympics in Seoul, South Korea. However, Pablo wasn't fast enough for the Olympic team.

Pablo went back to law school and continued training. He was ready to try again for the 1992 Olympics in Barcelona, Spain. There he reached his goal. He won the gold medal for the 100-metre butterfly race. Then he went on to win the gold for the 400-metre relay race, too. Pablo was overjoyed.

Pablo with his gold medal

Pablo with the relay team at the 1992 Olympics

Name:
Kristi Yamaguchi

Birthdate:
12th July 1971

Birthplace: Hayward,
California, United States

Sport: Figure Skating

Olympic Medals:
1 gold in 1992

Kristi Yamaguchi

Kristi Yamaguchi was born in 1971 in the United States. Kristi was born with feet that turned inwards. She had to wear plaster casts and special shoes to make them straight.

When Kristi was four years old her doctors said that she had to exercise to strengthen her legs. Her parents sent her to ballet classes.

When Kristi was five years old she saw Dorothy Hamill win the gold medal for ice skating at the Olympics. This inspired Kristi to take up ice skating, too.

By the time Kristi was eight years old her legs were much stronger. She loved skating so much that she woke up at four o'clock every morning. Then she got up and skated for five hours before school started.

Kristi's Inspiration

Kristi was inspired by Olympic skater Dorothy Hamill (above). She says, "Every little girl wanted to be just like Dorothy and I was no exception."

Kristi at the 1992 Olympics

Kristi and her friends in Central Park.

In 1983 Kristi started ice skating with a partner called Rudy Galindo. They made a very successful partnership and won many competitions together.

At the same time Kristi continued skating alone. She won many singles competitions, too.

Eventually Kristi had to make an important decision. She had to decide to continue skating alone or skate with her partner, Rudy, at the next Olympics. What should she do?

Kristi accepts the cheers of the crowd after winning the gold medal at the 1992 Winter Olympics.

Kristi skated alone in the 1992 Winter Olympics in Albertville, France. Before she went out on the ice she got a big surprise. Dorothy Hamill was backstage to wish her luck. Kristi was delighted and went out to skate her best.

Unfortunately Kristi fell when doing a difficult jump. However, she quickly got her balance and continued skating. Despite the unlucky fall, Kristi got the highest score. She won the gold medal and all her dreams came true.

Kristi won the gold medal at the 1992 Winter Olympics.

Olympic Sports

Ice sledge hockey is a popular sport in the Winter Paralympics.

All six of the Olympic champions worked hard to achieve their goals. They decided a a very young age which sport they would concentrate on. Most Olympic athletes compete in the Summer Games. However, there are the Winter Games, too. Which event would you choose to compete in?

Winter Games Sports

Olympics	Paralympics
biathlon (two events)	alpine skiing
bobsleigh	ice sledge hockey
curling	Nordic skiing
ice hockey	wheelchair curling
luge	
skating	
skiing	

Summary Games Sports

Olympics	Paralympics	
aquatics (includes diving and swimming)	archery	shooting
archery	athletics	swimming
badminton	boccia	table tennis
baseball	cycling	volleyball
basketball	equestrian (horse riding)	wheelchair basketball
boxing	football 5-a-side	wheelchair fencing
canoe	football 7-a-side	wheelchair rugby
cycling	goalball	wheelchair tennis
equestrian sports (horse riding)	judo	
fencing	powerlifting	
field hockey	sailing	
football		
gymnastics		
handball		
judo		
modern pentathlon (five events)		
rowing		
sailing		
shooting		
softball		
table tennis		
taekwondo		
tennis		
track and field		
triathlon (three events)		
volleyball		
weightlifting		
wrestling		

Index